POSITIVE
CHILDBIRTH
God's Plan
Practical Wisdom for Pregnancy & Delivery

Casey & Wendy Treat

ISBN#0-931697-57-3
Copyright © 1987 by Casey D. Treat and Wendy L. Treat
Reprinted 2004, 2010
Printed in U.S.A. 1987, 2004, 2010
All rights reserved under International Copyright Law.
Published by Casey Treat Ministries
P.O. Box 98800
Seattle, Washington 98198
www.caseytreat.com
www.wendytreat.com

TABLE OF CONTENTS

Foreword

Preface

1. Our Personal Testimony 13
2. God's Word on Childbirth 33
3. Children Are a Blessing 39
4. Are You in Agreement? 45
5. Confessing God's Word 55
6. Receiving Support from Others 69
7. Preparation is the Key 77
8. The Father's Role 91
9. Preparing For the Day of Birth 99
10. Dealing With Unexpected Circumstances . . 115
11. After Your Little One is Here 121
12. Entrusting Your Child to the Lord 131
13. Other Testimonies of Success 135

FOREWORD

We found ourselves first learning the Word concerning childbirth over twenty five years ago when we began our own personal experience with pregnancy, labor and delivery. Now, many years later we have changed, grown and renewed our minds, but the Word of God has stayed the same. The principles found in this book worked for us then, and they will work for you now.

One of the most important lessons we learned over the years is this: In all of our lives we have only one or two days (depending upon how many children you have) in which to enjoy this incredible experience of birthing our children. There are not many days that we want to live over and over, that we recall and talk about, photograph and video tape. But, the day we give birth to our children is top of the list of memorable occasions. Unfortunately, instead of enjoying it, we hurry through this amazing day to try and get it over with. Many of us go into this day with dread, and just pray for it to be over. We can't wait to be done.

We have all seen the women on TV yelling and screaming as they give birth, and we have thought of this as normal behavior. Yet this is the opposite of what will bring the best results in the birthing process. The Bible says the joy of the Lord is our strength. Concentrate on the joy of having your child, and your body will be able to relax and flow naturally.

God's Word is full of wisdom and power concerning childbirth. We believe you will have tremendous results in your pregnancy and delivery if you take the time to find out what the Word says, and make a decision to live God's Word daily. God wants to bless us with wonderful pregnancies, deliveries, and healthy, strong children. The result of a Christian couple becoming pregnant and giving birth to a child should always be good. The Bible says in James 1:17, *Every good gift and every perfect gift is from above, and comes down from the Father of lights, with whom there is no variation or shadow of turning.* God considers our children a good gift. He does not change His Word or His Will from person to person, or from situation to situation. God desires for each one of us to have the best in every area of our lives.

Romans 12:2 says, *And do not be conformed to this world, but be transformed by the renewing of your mind, that you may prove what is that good and acceptable and perfect will of God.* The world has taught and trained us to think contrary to the Word of God concerning childbirth. Whether you are pregnant right now or not, whether you are having your first child or your tenth, God's Word is true, and it will work for you. Renew your mind to God's Word and open yourself to learning God's ways. You can walk in His abundant blessing throughout pregnancy, labor, and delivery. Receive God's best!

CAUTION

This is not a professional opinion on pregnancy or childbirth. We are not saying you should do what we did. This is a Biblical approach to childbirth, with our testimony of how it worked for us.

PREFACE

We have truly experienced the abundant blessing and provision of God in our lives. As we have continued to walk in the promises of God day by day, we have found joy, peace, love, and fulfillment in every area. God's blessing has been more than we ever thought or imagined. We have found this to be especially true in the area of childbirth. The Word of God is full of wisdom, insight, and exciting promises for those who will seek the truth.

We would like to share with you our personal testimony about the births of our three children. Our son, Caleb, was born in June 1985, our daughter, Tasha, was born in April 1987, and our son Micah, was born in July 1989. We have relied upon God and His Word every step of the way. He has answered our prayers and blessed us abundantly. The Bible says in Ephesians 3:20, *Now to Him who is able to do exceeding abundantly above all that we ask or think, according to the power that works in us.* God has done exceeding abundantly more than we could have imagined in giving us our wonderful children. We know what God has done for us He will do for you!

Casey and Wendy Treat
Christian Faith Center
Seattle, Washington

CHAPTER 1

OUR PERSONAL TESTIMONY

CALEB - OUR FIRST GIFT FROM GOD

Casey's Day of Birth Testimony

On June 25, 1985, at 7:00am, as I was praying in the family room, I began to wonder when our child was going to be born. We didn't have a specific date, and since this was our first child, we had no idea what to expect. But in my spirit, I just felt it was time for the baby to come, so I began to pray for the birth process to begin. At that moment, Wendy was awakened by her water breaking. She came downstairs about 10 minutes later, interrupted my praying, and said, "I think my water just broke!"

I looked at her and said, "I'm sure it did! I was praying for the baby to come!"

We knew we had some time since she wasn't having contractions yet, so we decided to continue our normal routine for the day. I finished my prayer time and did the things I had to do at home. Of course, my insides were jumping, but I stayed calm. I went to the office at 8:30am, met with my scheduled appointments, and took care of business.

Next, I had a 10:30am class to teach, so at 10:15 a.m. I called Wendy. I could tell by her voice when she answered that something was happening. I said, "What's going on? How are you doing?"

She said, "We prayed that the baby would come when we are both here, so the baby can't come unless you're here."

I said, "I'll be right home." I went upstairs to the class and said, "I have some assignments for you." I was talking really cool. I handed out the outlines, summarized the class content, and reviewed what would transpire throughout the quarter. Then I said, "I'm sorry, but today I'm going to let you go early because Wendy's water broke, and I'm going home to have a baby." The class cried, cheered, and shouted.

When I got home at 11:00am, nothing much was happening, so we went for a walk. When we got back, we called the two friends who were going to help with the birth and asked them to come over. At this point, we prayed, talked, and listened to some music. Waiting and wondering when the baby would come was such a helpless feeling for me. I had prayed for the baby to be healthy, for Wendy to be strong, and for everything to go well, but I couldn't physically do anything. I just had to go through that time waiting for something to happen.

Then at about 3:30pm active contractions began. I could see that Wendy's body was working hard. We didn't know anything about breathing, since we didn't go through any classes, but her body responded, and she just flowed with it. Pretty soon we saw that she was almost ready to deliver. She was still walking around, a little slower than normal, of course, but walking.

We had put a thin mattress on the floor of our bedroom in preparation for the birth, so we had her lie down because the baby's head was right there, and we thought the baby would come immediately. As soon as Wendy laid down, she went to sleep! The rest of us just looked at each other and said, "This is definitely not what we want to happen!" The contractions had stopped, and she was sleeping quite soundly.

I gently shook her and said, "Wake up, we have to get this baby born!" She got back up and walked around some more. Then at about 4:30pm, we began getting down to business. Wendy pushed hard and worked with the contractions for around 45 minutes. Very soon, our son was born!

Caleb looked great when he came out. We patted him a little and held him and soon he squeaked. When I heard that squeak, I knew it was the greatest sound I had ever heard. Then he really started squawking and breathing. We cleaned out his mouth and nostrils, laid him on Wendy's stomach, and I said, "His name is Caleb Douglas Treat." We laid hands on him as we cried, thanked God, sang and prayed in tongues. It was the greatest day of my life.

About five minutes later I cut the umbilical cord, and then Wendy delivered the afterbirth. Wendy wanted to get right up and take a shower, so she jumped up, started across the room, and blacked out about half way across. We didn't realize the amount of energy and strength she had used. She waited a few minutes, then got up and took a shower. When she was done, we all gave Caleb a bath, took some video footage of him, and then had dinner.

The day of birth was one of the most exciting, emotional, and fun days I'll ever experience. The only thing that compares to it are the births of our other children. There was never any fear, worry, or anger. I remember someone telling me that Wendy might say some things she didn't mean while in the midst of giving birth. Everything she said was always good. She was making jokes, smiling and laughing. Not that it was easy. What I saw was equal to the hardest exercise program she ever went through, but she was never mad or screaming with pain. We trusted God. We prayed and worshipped, and everything went smoothly.

Wendy's Day of Birth Testimony

The morning of the day our son, Caleb, was born,

I was sleeping while Casey was downstairs praying. All of a sudden, at 7:00am, it was like a balloon popped inside of me. I walked downstairs thinking, "Is this it? I've never felt anything like this before." I walked very slowly into the room where Casey was praying and said, "Casey, I think my water broke."

He said excitedly, "I'm sure it did! I was praying for the baby to come."

I thought to myself, "Wow, it's today! The day is here; it's actually going to happen today." At this point, I was not really sure what to do. I wandered through the house a few times, and ate some breakfast. Then I decided to go for a walk outside. As I walked, I could feel some contractions, but they weren't painful or really strong at all. It just felt like a muscle tightening up. I wasn't sure if the contractions were really doing anything, since I had never had one.

When I got home I didn't know what to do. I felt restless, and I wanted something to start happening. There isn't much to do when you know your baby is going to be born, but you're not in active labor yet. There wasn't anyone to talk to because Casey had gone to work. I was restless, and I wanted things to get going. When Casey called, I said, "The baby is not going to come out until you are here, so why don't you come home and be with me?" We had been in agreement throughout the pregnancy that the baby would not come unless Casey was with me! So he came home right away, and we went for another walk.

As the birth continued I was able to stay relaxed and at peace because I was not full of fear. My body responded to the contractions naturally. When the contractions came, I automatically did the things that caused me to relax and help the birth process along. At one point, I laid down on the mattress we had prepared for the birth and fell asleep. When I woke up, I began to push some more. I remember seeing Casey and sensing how helpless he felt. One time I said, "Honey, you don't have to watch me. I promise, Casey, it's not bad. It's no big deal."

I continued to work with the contractions for

about 45 minutes, and then someone said, "Here he comes!" And he just came out. The emotion was just incredible. We wanted to laugh, cry, and jump. We were happy; we were relieved! All the emotions just came like a flood.

Casey put Caleb on my stomach and said, "His name is Caleb Douglas Treat!" After that, we cried with joy. Casey cut the umbilical cord, and then we spent some time in awe of our baby and in praise to God.

TASHA - OUR SECOND GIFT FROM GOD!

<u>Casey's Day of Birth Testimony</u>

Having experienced the birth of our son two years earlier, I was excited to meet our newest Treat. Wendy woke me up early in the morning of April 6th, and told me her water had just broke. I was excited, yet from our first birth experience I didn't think things would happen soon. I asked Wendy what she wanted me to do and she said just go back to sleep for awhile and that she would wake me when she felt like it was time to prepare.

The next thing I knew I heard her yelling from downstairs saying, "Casey, come now!" I jumped out of bed and took off downstairs. Wendy was sitting on the floor in the bathroom, so I thought I would try and move her to a more comfortable location. I wanted to get things ready but all I had time to do was grab a couple of towels and catch our beautiful red-headed girl as she made her way into the family!

I spent the next few minutes praising God and getting Wendy and our brand new daughter cleaned up and comfortable.

God's Word worked just the way we believed and confessed it would. Wendy did so great, and I know her confidence and reliance on the Word made this experience very special.

Wendy's Day of Birth Testimony

The birth of our second child, Tasha Suzanne, can only be described by Ephesians 3:20, *Now unto Him who is able to do exceeding abundantly above all that we ask or think, according to the power that works in us.* Tasha's birth was really beyond anything I could have asked or even thought.

The birth began when my water broke at 1:45am on Monday, April 6th. I woke up Casey and told him, but because of the way the birth progressed with Caleb, I told Casey to go back to sleep. I decided to go downstairs to pray and walk around for a while. After walking for a few minutes I began to have very strong contractions. I knew the contractions were really doing something, but I expected them to continue for quite a while. After six or seven good contractions I felt like I needed to push. I was still walking and praying and Casey was still upstairs sleeping. I got myself into a position where it was comfortable to push and realized that the baby's head was right there. I was ready to deliver!

I called Casey, and I knew he could tell by my tone that I meant, "Come right now!" He was downstairs in record time, and began running around trying to get things ready for the birth. I said, "I don't think you're going to have time for that. The baby is coming now!" He had just enough time to grab some towels and put them around me on the bathroom floor. After three pushes our beautiful little girl, Tasha Suzanne was born!

We had planned to have two of our friends over to help, but there just hadn't been time. When I asked Casey the time, it was 2:45am, just one hour from the time my water had broken! I am just in awe of what God has done for me. It was so much more than I could have ever imagined! We finally called one of our friends and said, "You had better come over and hold our little girl while we clean up!" This birth was just wonderful! I know that God's Word works, and His love and mercy are more than enough to help each one of us! Our little girl was perfect, healthy, and whole. I am so thankful to God for giving her to us.

MICAH - OUR THIRD GIFT FROM GOD!

Casey's Day of Birth Testimony

It's amazing how God is faithful to the Word we speak into our lives, and yet at the same time how each experience is so unique and special. As we found we were pregnant for the third time, we were excited and full of faith for what God would do.

I had seen how great Wendy did with being pregnant and giving birth to our children. I felt my job throughout the process was to be a support for her, and to do all I could to keep her strong emotionally. As we progressed, there were times when other women in the church would make comments to Wendy that put her into a place of feeling like she needed to measure up to what she had done in the past. They would say things like, "Can you beat your last birth time?" or "We'll see if that will happen again for you." It put a lot of pressure on her to feel she needed to perform.

One day she was very upset, and as we talked and prayed, I told her that she was giving birth to our child. She shouldn't feel she had to perform in any way. All we were going to focus on was having a healthy, whole, happy child. Nothing else really mattered. I wanted to reassure her, and take any outside pressure off of her to meet any expectation except the God plan for this birth.

We figured out that the baby should be born in August, but Wendy felt impressed as she prayed that the baby would be born in July. We just continued to pray and believe for God's timing and His will for this child.

I was not surprised when Wendy told me her water had broken and even though it was six weeks before her due date, we were confident and ready to see our new child. Again, once Wendy's water broke it, was very quick and peaceful. As we went through the birth process, I kept my focus on Wendy and her needs. I asked what I could do for her and how I could best assist her. Did she want me right with her, talking, quiet, touching, or not touching her?

As I focused on her needs, I saw that it brought

her peace and security to know that I was there and ready to do whatever she needed. I didn't have time to think about whether or not I was comfortable with anything that was happening. I just wanted to help her.

In no time at all, our new son was here. We rejoiced, called our friends and shared the great news of our newest addition to the family. The biggest thing I can say about the birth of our children is that as a strong team who love God and believe His Word, we have truly experienced His best in our lives!

Wendy's Day of Birth Testimony

Right from the beginning of our journey of adding children into our home, Casey said that he felt we would have two boys and one girl. So, when I found I was pregnant for the third time, I was confident we would have a boy this time.

God reminded me again of the Scripture in Ephesians 3:20, *Now unto Him who is able to do exceeding abundantly above all that we ask or think, ac-*

cording to the power that works in us. I knew God would honor His Word in this pregnancy.

As I prayed for our new little one, God very strongly impressed upon me that he would be born in July, even though my due date was the end of August. Right away I told Casey and one of my friends what I felt the Lord was telling me. As time progressed, I also felt that he would be born on a Wednesday. Again, I told Casey and my friend what I felt God was saying to me about this birth. I didn't know why God was showing me these details, but I just kept speaking the Word and believing for God's abundance.

Looking back, I realize that God was letting me know that even though our new son was to arrive six weeks early, He knew, and that it wasn't a problem. I knew the baby was okay because of the assurance I had from God through prayer and speaking the Word. I never confessed he would be born early, just healthy and at the perfect time.

Throughout the pregnancy, I had several women in the church say things to me that were difficult for me to deal with. They made comments like, "How are you going to beat your last birth?" They were not encouraging me to succeed; rather they seemed to be waiting for me to fail. I would go home and cry and talk to God. Being pregnant is emotional enough without added pressure from people who are skeptical or jealous. I knew that I couldn't do anything to make the baby come quickly other than confess God's Word and believe for His best.

I have a great husband, so when I told him about the situation he just listened and helped me put it into perspective. (Husbands are so important to our success!) Casey prayed with me and then he said, "This is our baby. We are not performing for anyone else. We are praying and believing for a child who is healthy and whole. That is what we are focusing on, not on how fast the birth is, or what other people think about it."

As I went into labor for the third time, I just knew God had a plan for this special day. The scripture from Ephesians 3:20 was flooding my heart and mind as I rested on His Word. Micah Douglas Treat was born on July 12, 1989 in just one hour and fifteen minutes. God is able to do exceedingly above all that we ask or think!

Chapter 2

GOD'S WORD ON CHILDBIRTH

We don't believe that anyone will go through their pregnancy and delivery exactly the way we did. It's impossible for two different couples to go through the exact same things when bringing a child into the world. But you can have the attitude that it is a positive, fun experience. You can handle it without fear, worry, or problems.

God designed us to have children. Genesis 1:31 says, *Then God saw everything that He had made, and indeed it was very good.* God created us as unique and special beings. Part of what He gave us was the ability to conceive and give birth to children. He specifically created us to have children, and when He was done, He said it was very good!

In Genesis 3, we find what happened when man and woman sinned. They bowed their knee to the devil and they disobeyed God's Word. In Genesis 3:16 it says, *To the woman He said: "I will greatly multiply your sorrow and your conception; In pain you shall bring forth children; Your desire shall be for your husband, and he shall rule over you."* When man and woman sinned and became submitted to the lordship of Satan, the curse came upon them.

Sorrow came into childbearing as a result of the sin that came into the human race. But in Galatians 3:13, we read, *Christ has redeemed us from the curse of the law.* The curse that came upon man and woman when they submitted to the devil has been broken through Jesus. Galatians 3:14 goes on to say, *That the blessing of Abraham might come upon the Gentiles in Christ Jesus, that we might receive the promise of the Spirit through faith.* You are redeemed from the curse when you accept Jesus; therefore, you have the right to expect a good pregnancy and birth experience.

Remember, we walk by faith, not by sight, so if we don't know or believe what God has given to us, the devil can put the results of the curse on us anyway. He is a liar, a thief, and a cheat, and he doesn't care if we've been redeemed from the curse or not. If he can, he will put the results of the curse upon us (Deuteronomy 28:15). We have to use our faith and say, "I'm not going to take that curse. I'm not going to accept it." By faith in Jesus, we can accept deliverance from the sorrow that came on women in childbearing.

1Timothy 2:15 says, *Nevertheless she will be saved in childbearing if they continue in faith, love, and holiness, with self-control.* She shall be saved. The word "saved" means delivered, protected, and spared. She shall be delivered, protected, and spared in childbearing. We've got a promise in the Word to stand on that says we don't have to live out the curse in our lives. We don't have to accept that curse as part of our lives. We have been spared. We have been redeemed from the curse, and that includes childbearing. God very clearly states what His will is for us in this verse, *"...she will be saved in childbearing."*

Deuteronomy 28:2 says, *And all these blessings shall come upon you and overtake you, because you obey the voice of the LORD your God.* Verses 4 and 8 say, *Blessed shall be the fruit of your body. The LORD will command the blessing on you in your storehouses and in all to which you set your hand, and He will bless you in the land which the LORD your God is giving you.* The Bible goes on to say in Deuteronomy 28:11, *And the LORD will grant you plenty of goods, in the fruit of your body.* And in Deuteronomy 7:13, *And He will love you and bless you and multiply you; He will also bless the fruit of your womb.*

We can see from these scriptures that God wants to bless us with good pregnancies and healthy, whole children. Anything else goes against what God says about it. We can stand on the Word of God and know we will be blessed. We can believe. We can expect. We can just demand to be blessed in pregnancy and to be blessed in childbirth. We don't have to accept the physical problems that can try to come upon us. We can believe the Word of God is true and allow God to bless us.

CHAPTER 3

CHILDREN ARE A BLESSING

Before making the decision to have children we knew we had some worldly thinking we needed to change. People around us had told us that children would mess up our lifestyle, slow us down, and take a lot of fun out of life. We believed that when we had children, there would be many things we couldn't do anymore, and people confirmed our thinking all the time with their negative attitudes. Therefore, we were reluctant to have children for several years. We would talk about it, and then we would say, "Yes, let's just keep praying about it. We'll let the Lord lead us and we will know when the time is right."

We had been married for over five years before we began to renew our minds about having children. We saw that many things the world said were perverted. If we would think the opposite of what the world said, we would get a pretty clear picture of what the truth was. If the world says childbirth is a very painful, miserable experience, it is probably an exciting, good experience. (We've all seen the television shows with the woman screaming in pain on the delivery table.) We began to see from the Word that we are redeemed from the curse of the law. We don't have to go through the things that the world is going through.

In the course of renewing our minds about having children, we had three girls come and live in our home for a month. It changed our whole outlook. We saw the reality that children are a blessing from God. We also saw that we could handle the responsibility. We realized that God knows the things that we don't know, and He is going to help us. We have learned that by being pastors. There have been many things we haven't known, but God has helped us.

In starting our church, and the many ministry projects and visions we have had, we haven't always known how they were going to work, but God has helped us to succeed. We realized if God has helped us to succeed in so many other areas, even though we didn't know everything about them, God could help us to succeed in having children and being parents. When we asked God to help us and give us wisdom in the areas we didn't know about, the fear and worry about raising children left.

Another thought many people have to change is in the area of believing in themselves. Many of us are not sure we like ourselves enough to take a chance on a child growing up to be just like us. That thought can be very frightening. We may think, "What if no one likes my child?" because we are not sure that anyone really likes us. We may not feel we can say like the Apostle Paul did, "Follow me." For many of us, it takes time to realize that we can like who we are. When we begin to see that we are okay and that people like us, we will begin to see we can also raise children. We will see that they can be happy, fulfilled people, and that other people will like them too. We will also see that they are a tremendous blessing to us, because we will look at them the way we look at ourselves - as wonderful creations of a loving Heavenly Father.

We had been convinced that there was no way for us to raise children to be happy, free, and to live a positive life. But we decided to operate in faith and follow the Word, instead of the world. That opened the door for us to get excited about having children. We were able to see that children really are a blessing from God.

As we made a decision to go for it, we put together a prayer asking God to give us a child. We said, "Lord, give us a healthy, strong child that will grow up to be happy, to serve You, and to live a long, satisfied life." We wrote down two or three scriptures, agreed in prayer and believed that we had received.

CHAPTER 4

ARE YOU IN AGREEMENT?

The first step to successfully having a child is to be in agreement with your mate. Matthew 18:18-20 says, *Assuredly, I say to you, whatever you bind on earth will be bound in heaven, and whatever you loose on earth will be loosed in heaven. Again I say to you that if two of you agree on earth concerning anything that they ask, it will be done for them by My Father in heaven. For where two or three are gathered together in My name, I am there in the midst of them.* Jesus gave us authority on the earth. We have the authority to live a godly life. But many of us miss out because we are not in agreement with those around us. We can't walk in the power of God and walk in strife at the same time. It is so important, that as a husband and wife, you recognize the necessity of being in agreement. The fact of the matter is, without being in agreement, you will miss out on many of the blessings God has provided.

We all need to realize that having a child does not mean the wife has a baby. It means you both are having a baby; you both have responsibility, and

you both have to be equally involved and commit-
ted. Someone said, "Marriage is each person giving
50%." No, it is each person giving 100%. If you will
give all that you can, you will have the very best
marriage relationship available in the Lord. That
is the attitude we had when we began preparing
to have a child. We decided we were going to give
100%, renew our minds, and go through whatever
changes we had to go through. We wanted to do
everything possible to help each other and help our
child.

You must both be willing to give your all in order
to have God's best. You must both be involved 100%
in the decision to have a child and in the many decisions that follow. You must walk in agreement with
each other before you will be able to raise a child.
Many people think having a child will make their
marriage stronger and closer. No! If your marriage
is not strong before you have a child, it will not
get strong because you have a child. If anything, it
will get weaker. Having children is for two people
who can live in agreement with one another, and

work together as a team through every situation that comes up. A strong, healthy marriage is the only good foundation for raising up godly children. Those in a strong marriage are made stronger by being in agreement with each other.

We have been asked if a couple must be in total agreement before they decide to have a child. First of all, if you are married, you have to realize that you could have a child at any time. Many people don't realize that. If you are married, and you are having intercourse, you could have a baby. You both need to recognize this possibility and make the decision that it would be okay. It has happened many times that the parents are shocked and upset to find out they have had an "accident" - as they call their child. Then they are frustrated and mad for the whole nine months of the pregnancy and for a good part of the child's life. They might not say they are mad to their child or to anyone else, but the attitude is always there. Many people have grown up being told, "You were our little accident." You can avoid the shock and upset if you will make a decision beforehand that if you get pregnant it will be all right.

If you are in a pregnancy right now that was not planned, you may want to get some counseling. You may need to get help dealing with some negative feelings about not wanting your baby. Don't lie about how you feel. You have to admit the truth to get help and overcome the feelings that are within you. But help is available, and God will help you turn this unexpected circumstance into a wonderful blessing.

If you are not pregnant now and you are not in agreement, you should not get pregnant until you have both made the decision that you are ready. At the same time, don't base your decision to have a child on whether or not you feel totally confident and able to handle every situation. In reality, there is no way you can be totally ready for a new child in your home. You can prepare to the best of your ability and do what you can, and then when the child comes you will be able to handle whatever situations come up. But the foundation is your decision to go for it. Then you can work together as a team.

Even though you have made the decision to have a child you may still have some butterflies and wonder, "Oh boy, are we ready for this?" You may not have total confidence in your ability, or you may wonder how you'll be able to do all these new things. But, if you have made a solid decision, your underlying feeling will be, "This is exciting! I don't know exactly how it's all going to work yet, but I can hardly wait to find out!" Then as you're preparing for the many decisions that will come up -- whether or not to nurse, where you're going to have the baby, who's going to deliver the baby -- you might not have all the answers, but you will have pre-determined that you will get into agreement and talk about those things together.

There are some things about which you need to talk and make decisions in advance. For example, you can't wait until your baby is hungry and crying, then decide how or what you're going to feed him. You should know ahead of time what you both believe so you can be in agreement and work together. There's nothing worse than being in the middle of a situation only to find out that the person you want to be in agreement with does not believe the same as you. Or having your partner "go along" with your decisions because they don't want to think about it and then have them say they didn't really believe it or want it that way in the first place.

We are talking about being in harmony and in one accord. Many of us try to avoid an issue or keep peace by saying we are in agreement. What we're really saying is, "Do what you want. I really don't care as long as you don't bug me about it." We say, "Yes, dear," when we really mean, "I don't care. Do whatever you want to do." The agreement we are talking about is when two believers come together, find out what the Word says about their situation, and then agree for it to come to pass. That means believing what you say you believe. It means thinking about it, talking about it, challenging yourself (and each other) to see if you really do believe it. If you will do that, you will see some powerful results. You will be able to help one another stand on the Word and be strong because you are in agreement. There is complete peace that comes when you are in agreement with the Word and with your spouse.

CHAPTER 5

CONFESSING GOD'S WORD

CHAPTER 5

CONFESSING GOD'S WORD

Because we have a relationship with God, we know He wants the best for us; therefore, we wanted Him involved in our decision to have a child. From the very first time we talked about having children, through the process of renewing our minds, and up to the actual birth and delivery of each of our children, we stood on God's Word. We went to the Word when we saw we needed to change our thinking about pregnancy and childbirth. We needed the Word in order to bring forth a vision of success.

As Christians, we cannot afford to overlook the power that is in God's Word. God's Word is the power that created the universe. More than that, it is the power that raised Jesus from the dead. It is the power that made it possible for us to be born again. Psalms, chapter one, states if you will delight in God's Word, whatever you do will prosper. Jesus and the Word are one (John 1:1, 14), so any answers that are needed can be found in the Word. The scriptures show us there is power in God's Word and all of that power has been given to us as believers.

We want to share with you the confession we used and the scriptures that are available to build your faith concerning pregnancy and childbirth. The Word of God is what will build your faith so you can be victorious in life (Romans 10:17). Don't overlook the Word -- in it is the power to bring success into your life!

CONFESSION

The Bible is full of scriptures which teach us about the affect our words have upon our lives. Proverbs 6:2 says, *You are snared by the words of your mouth; you are taken by the words of your mouth.* Proverbs 18:21 says, *Death and life are in the power of the tongue, and those who love it will eat its fruit.* In Mark 11:23, Jesus says, *For assuredly, I say to you, whoever says to this mountain, 'Be removed and be cast into the sea,' and does not doubt in his heart, but believes that those things he says will be done, he will have whatever he says.*

The confession we used was full of God's Word. You can use this one or revise it to make your own.

Your confession should be spoken at least once a day. As you continue to speak these positive, faith-filled words you will be building a vision of success for yourself and your child.

Thank you, Father, that we have a perfect, normal, healthy child and that You are forming our child. You will bring forth our child as You promised in Your Word. Our child is positioned properly, head first, face down, and will rotate as it should. I thank You that our child is the perfect size for my body and that our child will come forth precisely when You have planned. Father, our child is a gift from You, and I thank You that You are watching over our child at all times. I am glad that I can enjoy my pregnancy and be healthy and strong all the time. I will have painless contractions and a perfect, short, easy delivery. I thank You that our child and I are both the perfect size for each other, and I will not tear or have any negative effects from contractions or delivery. I take good care of my body, and I exercise every day to be strong and healthy. Our child is very good and easy to take care of. Our child is happy, smiling, pleasant-natured, intelligent, loving, kind, courageous, loves Jesus, and is full of life! I am glad that I can nurse our child. Nursing is a joy and a delight, and I will prosper in my body as I do it. Our little one sleeps soundly through the night and is alert during the day. Thank You, Father, in the name of Jesus!

GOD'S WORD FOR THE EXPECTANT MOTHER AND THOSE WANTING TO BECOME PREGNANT

I Timothy 2:15

Nevertheless she will be saved in childbearing if they continue in faith, love, and holiness, with self-control.

Exodus 23:26

None shall lose her young by miscarriage or be barren in our land; I will fulfill the number of your days.
(Amplified Bible)

Psalm 127:3

Behold, children are a heritage from the Lord, the fruit of the womb is His reward.

Deuteronomy 28:11

And the LORD will grant you plenty of goods, in the fruit of your body.

Psalm 147:13

He has blessed your children within you.

Isaiah 54:13

And all thy children shall be disciples – taught of the Lord [and obedient to His will]; and great shall be the peace and undisturbed composure of your children. (Amplified Bible)

Deuteronomy 7:9

Therefore know that the LORD your God, He is God, the faithful God who keeps covenant and mercy for a thousand generations with those who love Him and keep His commandments.

Deuteronomy 7:13   *He will love you and bless you and multiply you; He will also bless the fruit of your body....* (Amplified Bible)

Genesis 33:5   *The children whom God has graciously given your servant.*

Malachi 2:15   *And did not God make [you and your wife] one [flesh]? Did not One make you and preserve your spirit alive? And **why** did God make you two one? **BECAUSE HE SOUGHT A GODLY OFF-SPRING [FROM YOUR UNION].*** (Amplified Bible)

Genesis 3:16   *I will greatly multiply your sorrow and your conception; in pain you shall bring forth children....***BUT...**

Galatians 3:13   *Christ has redeemed us from the curse of the law, having become a curse for us!*

Hebrews 11:11	*By faith Sarah herself also received strength to conceive seed, and she bore a child when she was past the age, because she judged Him faithful who had promised.*
Isaiah 40:11	*He will... gently lead those who are with young.*
Exodus 1:19	*And the midwives said to Pharaoh, "Because the Hebrew women are not like the Egyptian women; for they are lively and give birth before the midwives come to them.*
Psalm 91:11	*For He shall give His angels charge over you, to keep you in all your ways.*
Proverbs 3:24	*When you lie down, you will not be afraid; yes, you will lie down and your sleep will be sweet.*

Deuteronomy 31:6	*Be strong and of good courage, do not fear nor be afraid of them; for the LORD your God, He is the One who goes with you. He will not leave you nor forsake you.*
Psalm 22:9	*But You are He who took Me out of the womb; you made Me trust while on My mother's breasts.*
Isaiah 59:21	*"As for Me," says the Lord, "this is My covenant with them: My Spirit who is upon you, and My words which I have put in your mouth, shall not depart from your mouth, nor from the mouth of your descendants, nor from the mouth of your descendants' descendants," says the Lord, "from this time and forevermore."*
Proverbs 14:23	*In all labor there is profit, but idle talk leads only to poverty.* (Amplified Bible)

Proverbs 31:17   *She girds herself with strength,*
                        [spiritual, mental and physical
                        fitness for her God-given task],
                        and makes her arms strong
                        and firm. (Amplified Bible)

Proverbs 31:25   *Strength and dignity are her*
                        clothing and her position is
                        strong and secure. She rejoic-
                        es over the future -- the latter
                        day or time to come [knowing
                        that she and her family are in
                        readiness for it]! (Amplified
                        Bible)

Isaiah 41:10   *Fear not: [there is nothing to*
                        fear] for I am with you; do not
                        look around you in terror and
                        be dismayed, for I am your
                        God. I will strengthen and
                        harden you [to difficulties];
                        yes, I will help you; yes, I will
                        hold you up and retain you
                        with My victorious right hand
                        of rightness and justice.
                        (Amplified Bible)

II Timothy 1:7   *For God has not given us a*
                              spirit of fear, but of power and
                              of love and of a sound mind.

Romans 4:21   *...and being fully convinced*
                              that what He had promised He
                              was also able to perform.

Proverbs 11:21   *...the posterity of the righteous*
                              will be delivered.

Isaiah 44:3   *I will pour My Spirit on your*
                              descendants, and My blessing
                              on your offspring.

Isaiah 44:24   *Thus says the Lord, your Re-*
                              deemer, and He who formed
                              you from the womb.
                              (Amplified Bible)

Galatians 1:15   *But when it pleased God,*
                              who separated me from my
                              mother's womb and called me
                              through His grace.

Jeremiah 1:5a   *Before I formed you in the
                         womb I knew you; before you
                         were born I sanctified you.*

Isaiah 66:9   *"Shall I bring to the time of
                         birth, and not cause delivery?"
                         says the Lord. "Shall I who
                         cause delivery shut up the
                         womb?" says your God.*

Psalm 71:6   *By You I have been upheld
                         from birth; you are He who
                         took me out of my mother's
                         womb. My praise shall be con-
                         tinually of You!*

Deuteronomy 28:4   *Blessed shall be the fruit of
                         your body.*

CHAPTER 6

RECEIVING
SUPPORT
FROM OTHERS

Receiving support from others is a very important part of having children. The Bible tells us in Titus 2:3-5, *The older women likewise, that they be reverent in behavior, not slanderers, not given to much wine, teachers of good things -- that they admonish the young women to love their husbands, to love their children, to be discreet, chaste, homemakers, good, obedient to their own husbands, that the word of God may not be blasphemed.*

It is uncommon among people today to ask others who are experienced in certain areas but who are not "professionals" how to do something. The average person who wants to know about childbirth or pregnancy will go to the doctor. The doctor may have never had a baby. Doctors may rely only on what they have been taught at school, and may only be able to give the professional knowledge they have. But the problems we have usually don't come from a lack of professional knowledge; they are a result of not knowing how to deal with the emotions and attitudes that come up during pregnancy.

Our bodies will always follow our minds. When our minds are thinking sick, our bodies are going to get sick. The way we set our minds will control the way our bodies are going to react. It's the same way in pregnancy – if we think about something long enough, we will create it. You can create a good feeling in your body, or you can create discomfort; you can create a peaceful, easy delivery, or you can create problems. You can go whichever way you want, because your body will always follow your mind. The Word says, *For as he (she) thinks in his (her) heart, so is he (she)* (Proverbs 23:7), and that is also true in pregnancy.

In Titus, the Word teaches us that we're supposed to train each other. We are to go to the elder men and elder women, and they are to show us how to be successful: how to have a good home, how to take care of our children, and how to love our mates. But because we haven't done what the Word says, we have gone through unnecessary problems. We have gone through difficulties because we have followed professional opinion when it wasn't always the best way. Many times the professionals do not know the Word of God. They don't know that we have a higher authority and a higher goal. That is when we need to support, uplift, and train one another in what the Word says.

We cannot offer you any professional opinions, but we can testify and share some things we've learned from the Word and some things we've learned from experience. Our goal is to go God's way, not just the way of scientific knowledge. People were having babies long before doctors got involved, and people continue to have babies everyday around the world -- with and without medical doctors. Childbirth is very natural, and should be an easy process, especially when you know God and His ways.

Remember to challenge things that come up medically. Challenge why you are doing it, why you believe it, and why others have done it. If you think it's okay, then confirm it with someone who knows the Word. You should ask several people around

you. Proverbs 11:14 says, *Where there is no coun-
sel, the people fall; but in the multitude of counsel-
ors there is safety.* Be sure to ask people of faith
(these are the men and women to whom Titus was
referring), and see if they are in agreement with
you.

We are all members of the body of Christ, the
family of God. Open up and share yourself with others. If you don't ask, you may not find out there is a
better way. The Bible says in Luke 11:9-10, *So I say
to you, ask, and it will be given to you; seek, and
you will find; knock, and it will be opened to you.
For everyone who asks receives, and he who seeks
finds, and to him who knocks it will be opened.*

Open yourself up to Christian friends around
you. Ask for the support and wisdom you need.
If you don't have peace inside about something
you've heard or been told, ask someone who you
know follows the Word of God. Don't keep fear
and worry to yourself. You'll find that most fears,
worries, and problems can be solved very quickly.
Many times, simply sharing the worry will take

care of the problem.

God has given us other people to help build us up. He has placed each of us in the Body of Christ to help others and to receive help when we need it. First Corinthians 12:20, 21 says, *But now indeed there are many members, yet one body. And the eye cannot say to the hand, I have no need of you; nor again the head to the feet, I have no need of you.* We all have different needs at times. God says the way to have those needs met is through the Christian friends around us. Find friends with whom you can share, then allow the Spirit of God to meet your need through their love, wisdom, and support.

CHAPTER 7

PREPARATION IS THE KEY

When Wendy became pregnant, we were already in the mode of raising a child. We did not think, "In nine months, we are going to start raising a child." Before we knew for a fact that she was pregnant, we started renewing our minds about having children. We listened to teaching and studied the Word. We were training ourselves to be parents. We spoke the Word over our children throughout each individual pregnancy while they were still in the womb.

From the time Wendy realized she was pregnant, we began calling each of our children healthy and whole, wise, loving, kind, and blessed of God. We spoke the Word over them all the months they were developing. We have always said our children would come forth easily. There would be no pain or suffering, no misery or problems. And Wendy would have an easy, fast delivery.

Oftentimes people wait until their child comes and then wonder, "What are we going to do now?" You need to be a parent *before* you give birth. You have been given nine months to train yourself as a parent. If you use that time wisely, you will have a head start on the many things you need to learn. The moment you become pregnant you need to recognize that **you are a parent.** You don't just become a parent the day your baby is born. Your children are just as much your children in the womb as they are once they are physically born. As you begin talking about the responsibilities of becoming parents, you will develop a vision that you **are** a mom and a dad long before anyone can physically see that you are parents.

In preparing to become parents we also watched other people. We watched how they reacted and responded to their children. We watched how they held the babies. We both went into the daycare at the church to become familiar with changing diapers, giving baths, feeding, and all the many things you need to know about caring for babies. We wanted to prepare ourselves to be the very best parents we could be. We didn't want to be caught off guard, so we thought of ways that we could learn as much as possible to help us. The pregnancy was a time of careful, well-thought-out preparation for us. And it was a great benefit to us once our little ones were actually here.

MORNING SICKNESS

There is one thing that I feel is important to mention about my pregnancies. In all of my pregnancies, I never dealt with morning sickness. I think that because my mom set such a strong example of not allowing sickness into our household, I just never get sick. So when it came to pregnancy, I didn't see it as normal to become sick.

The Bible says that Jesus redeemed us from the curse. Part of the curse that Jesus redeemed us from is physical sickness. Pregnancy should be a time of joy and celebration, not sickness and pain. When we stand on God's Word we can go through all of our pregnancy healthy and free from feelings of sickness.

What happens with most women is they do not know the promises of God, and that they can be healthy for their whole pregnancy. They allow morning sickness to control the first few months of their pregnancy.

I am not saying that there aren't physical changes that happen during pregnancy. When you are pregnant, your body is definitely going through some major changes. You are supporting a new life, and all that it takes to create and give birth to that new life. I did have times when I needed extra rest, and I took care to eat right and exercise properly. But, I did not plan to be sick, and I was not sick.

If you have had a problem with morning sickness during previous pregnancies, do some smart things for yourself in your next pregnancy. Go to a nutritionalist or the health food store, get vitamins or supplements, and learn about specific healthy things you can do to help alleviate the symptoms. Then speak the Word over your body. Don't just allow yourself to be sick because you think it is normal. Even though it has become acceptable in our current society, it is not God's best to experience morning sickness.

Exercise is an important part of preparing

yourself for the birth of your child. It is a fact that your pregnancy and delivery will be much easier if you exercise before you become pregnant. You should be physically fit to have a baby. Childbirth is hard work, and a good exercise program will pay off in the long run. You'll feel better throughout your whole pregnancy, and the benefits will show up when it's time to deliver.

I have consistently exercised my body all of my adult life, and I know that my commitment to exercise is part of the reason my pregnancies and deliveries were so good. I exercised regularly until the day each of our children were born, and started again within a few days afterwards. I believe that many of the problems, such as backaches, fatigue, and even swelling can be eliminated or at least reduced considerably through proper exercise. You'll not only physically strengthen your body; you will also get a great deal of satisfaction and self-worth from disciplining yourself.

Remember to be wise when exercising. If you have not exercised up to this point, do not go out and try to run a marathon. You need to start realistically and even walking a mile or two every day will help you. Do what you can and start where **you** are, but do something. You'll be amazed at what a difference it will make!

One good book I can recommend on exercise and good health is, Greater Health God's Way by Stormie Omartian. This is an excellent book. It is also much more thorough than I can be in a book of this type.

Weight gain is a big area of discussion among pregnant women. It seems to be something women use as a matter of competition, and also something about which we feel bad. If we are the ones who gained the most weight, we can really feel bad. You have to decide that you are a disciplined woman of God, therefore you will not worry about the amount of weight you gain during pregnancy. Now, if you are going to eat three pieces of cheesecake every day and pig out on all kinds of fattening foods, you should worry about how much weight you are gaining. You must determine that you will eat sensibly, exercise, and take good care of your body so you won't think badly about gaining weight. You can use the will God gave you to determine to be disciplined, and believe God for the results you want for your pregnancy, delivery, **and** getting back into shape. (I personally gained fifty pounds with each of my children, and I was back in shape within six months.) You don't have to accept stretch marks, permanent weight gain, or even a long recovery time to get back into shape. Just believe God and discipline yourself to receive the results you want.

Another area that goes along with weight gain is how you think about your body changing. I had been heavy all my life, but I had been exercising and successfully working with my weight for several years before getting pregnant. Even though I felt I was just the way I wanted to be, I still had to work with my thinking as my body began to change.

One day a friend of mine said, "You're already getting bigger." I quickly came back with, "Oh no, I'm not." She said, "You know, your body is going to be getting bigger and you can't feel bad about that."

I quickly said, "Oh, I don't. I feel good about it."
She restated my comment about not getting bigger, and I had to look at the fact that those inches
I had taken off around my mid-section were going
to come back. So I made a decision that I was going
to love the way I looked. That doesn't mean I didn't
have to bite my tongue. Sometimes, I wanted to say,
"Look at this! I'm huge and I don't fit in any of my
clothes!" Inside, I just wanted to cry. It was a very
real emotion. But we cannot let emotions change
the decision we have made to feel good about our
bodies during pregnancy. We cannot feel badly
about the bodies that are carrying our children. It
is well worth anything we go through physically to
give birth to our wonderful children.

The main thing to remember is not to use pregnancy as an excuse to change your eating habits
for the worse. Don't get lazy. Stay disciplined and
consistent. The old myths that you are "eating for
two," and that you will have wild cravings are simply not true (unless it is something your body real-

ly needs). You can use your pregnancy as an excuse to eat more than normal, but after the baby is born you will have to deal with the results. If you will decide to eat right, exercise, and not worry about how much weight you will gain, it will come right off again. Then you will be able to enjoy both your pregnancy and getting back into shape.

SEX: DURING AND AFTER PREGNANCY

When a woman is pregnant she can still have sex. She doesn't lose all of her sex drive, and her husband doesn't either. What many couples forget to do, or won't do is to communicate about the changes that are going on. You have to communicate about the changes that come up as your pregnancy progresses. For the first few months, there is no difference. Even up to the fourth or fifth month there is still not much difference. When you get up to the sixth and on through the eighth month, you have to start changing some things. You need to communicate about how you, as a couple, can satisfy each other's need for physical contact and sexual love. During the last few weeks, men, you are going to have to be aware of your wife's needs. Let her know that you love her, and if you need to, put sex on hold until later; set it aside for a few weeks even until after the baby's arrival.Communication is the key. You are just going to have to communicate. Women should not have to say, "Okay, I'm going to have to tough it out right now to try to please my husband." You both should work together and communicate. Be open about it; there is no sense in putting yourselves through turmoil. If you both want to help each other and meet each other's needs, you won't have a problem.

Many times re-establishing a sexual relationship after the baby is born is delayed by the wife thinking it might hurt her. There usually isn't a reason you physically can't have sex, but after having a baby it takes a little time to get back to normal. The wife may cower away until she realizes it's okay, that it really doesn't hurt. This is why communication is so important. The husband can help his wife by talking gently, sharing kind words of encouragement, and by doing thoughtful acts for her during this important time. Gentleness and taking extra time will be a real benefit to reestablishing your sexual relationship. Eventually her body will get back to normal, and everything will be wonderful.

Another thing that can hold you back from sexual intercourse after the baby arrives is not having anything planned for birth control. Make a decision on the type of birth control you will use before the need comes up. Then you can relax and not hold back physically from your mate.

Remember to stay sexually and romantically involved with one another. It is so important to communicate and talk about the different changes that you are both experiencing. It may not be the same as before pregnancy, but that doesn't mean you won't enjoy it. If you love each other, you will continue to express it physically, and you will enjoy your sexual relationship until a few weeks before delivery, and you will become sexually involved again within a few weeks afterwards. Remember, having sex is not just coming to a climax; it is a celebration of love.

CHAPTER 8

THE FATHER'S ROLE

As a husband, there is much you can do to help your wife during pregnancy. Your words can build her up or tear her down. Because of the changes that happen in their bodies, many women talk negatively about themselves. They begin to say things like, "Gee, I can't get into bed, I can't get out of bed. These dumb nylons won't stay up. I can't walk normally." You can make these things fun, light and positive! For example, you can say, "It's watch-mom-put-on-her-nylons time!" Remember though, laugh at the changes going on, not at her, her body, or the problems. Her body is going to change, but you can help keep her mind from thinking about it negatively.

You can build up your wife with actions as well as words. Look for ways to meet her needs and make her feel good. When Wendy was about seven or eight months pregnant, she was having a hard time finding clothes that fit. We went into the maternity store and I told her to go into a changing booth. I said, "You're not coming out until we find something for you to wear." Then I went out to the racks, and I took everything to her that I thought might be nice. I'd go back out and look for more while she was trying on a few items.

She would say, "Nothing's going to work," and I knew she just wanted to cry. I would say, "It's okay, there's still more to try on." When we left, she had two or three things that she could wear. What's important about this incident is that Wendy felt better. It isn't that we spent a lot of money, but that I helped meet her needs. I was looking for ways to encourage her.

Sometimes as men, we don't realize what's important to our wives. Don't let your wife get into situations where she's going to get depressed, get her feelings hurt, or worry about things. Take charge, and do something to make a change. Don't just say, "You'll get over it, you only have a month to go." Help her!

Another thing I did was have pictures taken. I wanted pictures of Wendy, just before we had our child, with all nine months showing. I knew Wendy wasn't going to look like that very many times, and

I wanted a really nice picture of her. So we had our picture taken professionally. I look at those pictures now, and I love them. That was just another special way of building her up and saying, "You're beautiful! I like how you look." Men, I encourage you to find ways to show this kind of love to your wife.

I read some books and gathered information for Wendy. I found positive, uplifting information for her and gave that to her. God does not write about everything that could go wrong. He tells us how to overcome in every situation.

Husbands also have the responsibility to help deal with other people. If there are people who do not agree with what you are doing, don't get involved in conversations about it with them. On the other hand, do not say things to stir people up. We never announced that we were going to have our baby at home. When people came to us with negative comments we just said, "That's not what we believe," and left it at that. When you are strong in what you believe, people quiet down quickly. They know you are not open to conversation about it. Don't try to change them because they have their own beliefs. If someone wants you to share with them what the Word says, that's one thing, but trying to convince people who don't want to learn is very unwise.

There were times when Wendy would be exposed to negative stories or conversations, and I would have to help her out of the situation. There were also times when she would help me with what I was hearing. We worked together as a team. Men, as the head of your household, you need to be very involved, and if necessary, take charge to protect and guard your wife's heart.

One thing to remember is that you don't want to avoid hearing things because you are afraid if you do, something bad might happen. If that is your attitude, then you are going to be in trouble. Second Timothy 1:7 says, *For God has not given us the spirit of fear; but of power, and of love, and of a sound mind.* I did not let Wendy or myself listen to negative things because I'm just not interested in hearing about them. I'm interested in hearing what God has to say. Those are the things that will help us to be successful.

As men, the main thing for us to do is build up, encourage, and support our wives. We need to be as involved during the pregnancy and birth of our children as we possibly can. In the world, we have been trained to let the women handle almost everything to do with childbirth. As godly men, we need to be involved in every aspect of the pregnancy and birthing experience. We need to know what is going on with our wives. Ask the Holy Spirit to help you give to your wife. He will show you creative ways to share your love with her and ways for you both to share in this special time together.

CHAPTER 9

PREPARING FOR
THE DAY OF BIRTH

GOD'S TIMING IS PERFECT!

Many women get frustrated towards the end of their pregnancy because they have focused on a "due" date, instead of the One Who promised to bring forth their child when the time was right. Relax and allow God to work in you. He has a plan, and He knows better than you do when your child is perfectly ready to come forth.

When I first found out I was pregnant with Caleb, I was told a day that I would deliver. He wasn't born on that day. The midwife also gave me a date, and Caleb wasn't born on that day either. He was born on the day he was ready to be born. I think it is very unwise to put into your head that your baby has to come on a particular day. You need to remember, God is in control of your labor and delivery. His timing is perfect. Put your trust in God and His Word, and you won't get frustrated if a particular date comes and goes without your baby being born. Trust that God wants the best for you and your child, and let peace prevail throughout your whole pregnancy.

PLANNING FOR DELIVERY

The two most important decisions you must make after you become pregnant are **where** you will have the baby, and **who** will help you deliver the baby. There are several choices available to you today. There are hospitals, birthing rooms in the hospital, birthing clinics, and home births. You need to check out each alternative and decide which is best for you. This is a major decision, and you should not wait until the last few weeks to settle it. You need to have your mind focused on where you're going to have your baby. Whether it's at home, the birthing center, or at someone else's home, you need to make a firm decision where it will be. Then, you can plan and mentally visualize the birth. And when the time comes, you'll be ready.

If you do not take the time to plan you can end up like those who panic while trying to find the suitcase to get to the hospital in time. They panic because they have never really thought through what they will do when the baby comes. When you have a vision, things will go smoothly. You simply and calmly do what you've already planned. The plan is in your mind, and your body will follow your mind, so everything goes the way it should. It is particularly important for the woman to know where she wants to have the baby. She is the one who will be doing the work, and she needs to be comfortable, relaxed, and able to concentrate. Of course, both husband and wife must feel confident about the decision, but the wife will have to feel most secure in this decision.

If you do not make these decisions, you leave yourself in a position to allow room for fear or bad feelings. You may end up doing something you don't want to do. One couple we know never made a decision, so they ended up going to the hospital. As soon as their baby was born, they wanted to go home. The hospital staff threw a fit. They said, "You can't leave. You are under our protective care and you have to stay until we release you." These parents went through a lot of stress. There they were with a newborn baby, and they were fighting

with the hospital staff. They were upset and frustrated, all because they had not made the decision
beforehand of what they would do when their baby
was born.

Before we became pregnant, we prayed, medi-
tated on the Word, and sought God for His direc-
tion in the birth and raising of our children. The
decision to have our first child at home was easy
because we had been seeking God. We didn't wa-
ver back and forth, and wonder if we should or
should not have our child at home. The thoughts,
"I'm scared," or "What if we have a problem?" did
not enter our minds. The decision was easy, but
it was reached through a process of building our
faith over a period of months. We also spent time
talking with other people about what we wanted to
do.

Although in the beginning, we had assumed we
would go to the hospital, as the pregnancy continued, we began to see that maybe this was not God's
best for us. We already knew we were going to walk
in faith and that God had promised we could be

blessed in childbirth. But we finally came to the decision that we didn't want to have our baby in a hospital, mainly because of the many Caesarean sections being done at the hospital. Time after time, our friends went into the hospital for a "normal" delivery, and they came home having had C-sections.

We knew we were not open to having a C-section, so we decided not to put ourselves in a position to allow for that possibility. We also knew that as soon as the baby was born, the hospital staff would want to give him a Vitamin K shot, give him some antibiotic drops, do a blood test on him, and various other medical functions. All of this would be done within the first few minutes after the child was born. Before we could have said anything to stop them, everything would have already been done.

We really challenged ourselves to make sure having our child at home was what we wanted to do. We found we were completely comfortable with our decision. (We knew neither one of us could go through this if we were in fear! We had to be full of faith and excitement.) Since the decision to have our child at home was a well-thought-out process, once we made the decision, there was no fear or worry about it. It was the natural, normal thing for us to do. For us, there were no other options. This was the decision that brought us peace and allowed us to operate in faith.

We knew that having our child at home was the right decision **for us**. It is very important for you to understand this. Don't decide to have your child at home because of what someone else did. You need to personally prepare yourselves and know what you want to do as a couple. Both husband and wife need to be at peace and in agreement. Then you will be able to operate in faith and know God's peace is working in you!

I would like you to look at your decision of where to have the baby from another angle. Some people have come to me and said, "Wow! Wendy, you really have big faith." There are many women who have had babies at home. The majority of women outside the United States do not have their babies in the hospital. So don't try to figure out if you have enough faith or not. There are many people who don't have any faith in God, and they have their babies at home every day. It really has more to do with what you want to do, than how much faith you have. Your decision must line up with what you and your mate can agree upon and are both comfortable with. You cannot decide to have your child at home just because someone else said that is the way you should do it. The question is: What do **you** want to do? Make your decision, feel good about it, and everything else will flow.

The other decision you need to make is **who** will help you with the delivery. Someone has to be there: a doctor, a midwife, or someone who has had experience with childbirth. Find someone you can trust and in whom you have confidence. Remember, you don't need to be fearful of doctors. When we teach about trusting the Lord, we're not talking about being afraid of doctors. We're saying **trust the Lord.** If you're going to go to doctors to ask for their help, they're going to tell you what they know in the natural - what they've studied and what they've learned. If you choose to go to them do not be upset with everything they tell you. If you squabble over everything they say, then you put them in a bad situation. They are responsible to give you their best professional input. That's what they're trained to do. If you are going to reject their professional input, and try to tell them what God says about it every time they tell you something, then there's no sense in going to them. What we are saying is, don't decide to go to a doctor, and then try to make him "renew his mind" throughout your pregnancy.

If I wanted to go to the doctor, I would go to him and say, "Doctor, I would really like to have this child naturally. How could you help me with that?" I would explain exactly what I wanted to do, and then see how he could work with me. If he is a good doctor, he will explain everything he can do to help you. Then you're going to have to decide if you can work with him. Don't just go to a doctor, walk into the office and say, "Here I am. Here's my money. Do whatever you want with me." You are hiring the doctor to serve you. You need to interview him or her and decide if they are the best person to meet your needs. One way to find a good doctor is to ask other people who they recommend. Find out who they go to and why they chose them.

Another possibility is for a midwife to deliver your child in your home. It is becoming more and more common for people to have a midwife come into their home to deliver their child. The same principles apply when choosing a midwife. You are hiring them so don't just settle for the first one you meet. Be selective and be sensitive to the Holy Spirit's leading as a couple. We believe that through prayer and seeking the Lord, you will make the decision that will be best for you.

Because we had chosen to have our child at home, and since we didn't know anything about the birthing process, we needed someone with us who did. After prayerful consideration, we asked two women to be with us during the delivery. One was a nurse who was a woman of faith and prayer, and the other was a friend who was experienced in home deliveries. To make sure we all knew what to expect, we set up a time to talk about exactly what we would do on the day of birth. We were in harmony about what we believed would happen, and what responsibilities each person would have. We were prepared, and we were in agreement.

Whomever you choose to be with you when you deliver, make sure you communicate with them. Don't leave anything to chance or tell them what you want them to do in the midst of the birth. That is not the time to try to talk about things. You want to be sure to understand each other and be in agreement before you go into labor.

LABOR AND DELIVERY

In talking about the actual birthing process, "pain" is the word many people use to describe it. When I think of pain, I think of falling down on the gravel and skinning my knee. I would be in some pain. It would hurt. But when my body is expanding and going through the changes it takes to birth a baby, I would rather call that "travail." Galatians tells us that there is travail in childbirth. Travail means to work hard. You're going to have to go through some discomfort in getting the baby out of your body. But you don't have to suffer and be miserable.

Actual labor and delivery is an area that causes a lot of discussion among women. Whose labor was the best? Whose was the shortest? Whose was the longest? Who did it "naturally" and who did not? If we are using faith to believe for God's best, discussions like this can really dishearten us. We can hear about how someone else had a very short labor, and then if our labor goes on for more than two hours we wonder how we "missed it."

I once spoke with a woman who told me how disappointed she was in her labor and delivery. After talking to her for a while, I realized that she had successfully given birth to her child naturally. The problem was that it took her 30 hours of labor to bring forth her child. She was seriously questioning her "faith" and wondering why that had happened. She was also planting seeds of fear and doubt about her next pregnancy. I shared with her how she had actually won! It might have been a longer time than what she had wanted, but she had stuck with her decision to have her baby naturally. In that situation, it is often easier to go the quick way and just get it over. So even though she had to work and stand on the Word for a very long time, she got the end result of a natural birth.

The Bible is very clear about God's will. His desire is for us to have the best. Therefore, we can believe and expect for His best in our lives. Giving birth naturally to your child is a joyful, wonderful experience. The Bible says the Hebrew women delivered very quickly (Exodus 1:19). If God desired quick, lively deliveries for the Hebrew women, He has the same desire for you.

Our role is to renew our minds, to confess the Word, to pray and believe for God's best. We can't compare ourselves with what someone else has done. We look at other people for an example and a higher vision, not to condemn ourselves and feel bad if we don't do it exactly as they did. We aim for the best in what we can do, and don't judge, condemn, or compare ourselves if we don't think we reached our perfect goal. Remember, our perfect goal is a strong, healthy child, and a strong, healthy mom. You are special, and God is working in you to do His perfect will in your life.

Another area which you may need to renew your mind about is the actual delivery. You may wonder, "Will I measure up?" "Can I do it?" or "What if someone sees me, and I look funny?" These thoughts can go through your mind and make you nervous. You have to come against those negative thoughts, and tell yourself that you're going to do just fine.

Now, you won't get everything solved in the first week, because thoughts will come up at different times throughout your pregnancy. But as they come up, talk with your husband and your friends, and pray about it. Realize that you can do it! Prepare your body with exercise, your spirit with God's

Word, and prayer; then believe God for the rest. He will never leave you or forsake you, and He's right there ready to help bring forth your child.

CHAPTER 10

DEALING WITH
UNEXPECTED CIRCUMSTANCES

Many people get into condemnation when their pregnancy or birth experience doesn't go exactly the way they had planned or believed. If you have had situations during your pregnancy or birth experience that haven't gone the way you had hoped, just praise God that you had the medical attention you needed. Believe that the next time you will be more prepared. There is a perfect mark for which we are shooting, and although we may get close, we don't always hit the center of the target.

Make the decision that you are going to follow God's Word, be disciplined, and ask God to show you areas you can change. As He reveals these areas to you, be obedient to change. You'll then be able to move on in faith, believing for God's best. Thank the Lord that you have a child. How that baby came forth doesn't change the child. If you get caught up with thinking about how you failed, you won't be able to go on in faith and believe the best for your child.

A woman once told me she was having morning sickness, and she was feeling badly about it. She felt it was because her faith was not strong enough. I said, "Wait a minute, slow down. You're going to get yourself so wound up about not having enough faith that you'll open yourself up for other things to happen. Just be smart. Get extra rest if you need it, and find out what kinds of foods are best for you to eat in the morning." She changed some of her eating habits, stopped feeling bad, got some extra rest, and she was doing great. Had she continued to feel bad by thinking she didn't have enough faith, she would have made things worse.

Remember, whatever has happened or whatever does happen, love is the key. You might not do anything that we say or that we did, but if you have the love of God coming out of you, then your child is going to be fine. The Bible says that love covers a multitude of sin; love covers a multitude of mistakes. Remember, whatever you go through, if you keep love flowing from you to your husband and your child, then you're going to be all right. Everything's going to come out fine. Don't get into a legalistic "I-did-it-wrong" mentality. Stay in love.

Of course, there is a "right way" to do things, and that's where we should aim. We should always aim for the best, but when we don't hit the bull's-eye, we shouldn't kick ourselves – just keep walking in love. We believe that what we teach won't put anyone in bondage or condemnation, but rather it will present a mark to shoot for according to God's Word. If we're aiming for the bull's-eye and get one line outside of it, we can still praise God we hit the target. The next time we'll be an even better shot. We may go through some things we didn't expect, but we still need to aim for the perfect mark.

The devil will always bring thoughts of how you didn't do enough or of how you don't have enough faith. He'll use anything he can to bring fear and doubt into your mind. You have to cast those thoughts down and not let anything – television, books, advertisements – feed those thoughts. Also, don't listen to people who want to tell you about situations that didn't work out for the best. Realize these negatives do affect you, and keep your mind clear and fixed on your goal.

Whether it is the birth of your child, nursing, healing -- or any other area of your life -- you have to guard yourself. Protect your ears, watch your words, and don't get caught up in what others think about you. When you are going for God's best you may have to stop people from saying what they want to say. If you don't, you plant the wrong vision in your heart, and you will not be strong in standing in faith for the best. Remember, we are talking about aiming for the perfect mark and going for all that God has provided.

CHAPTER 11

AFTER YOUR LITTLE
ONE IS HERE

You have made many decisions so far, such as who will help you deliver the baby, and where to have the baby. Now the time has come to make another decision. You need to think about who is in charge of the house: you or the baby. We have seen many new parents stop their ministry activities, fellowship, social life, and even their sex life. The baby takes complete control of their lives, and they begin to "serve" the baby. Now, of course, the baby does have needs that must be met, but you must decide how and when to meet those needs. You don't have to be awake all night with your baby. You may need to feed them once during the night, but other than that, they should be asleep at night and awake during the day. We have all accepted as fact that we must be awake half the night with our newborn babies. Many people have gone so far as to carry this behavior on for years. They have worn themselves out and accepted it as normal.

Children should not be allowed to turn the house and family upside down. You don't have to stop all your fellowship or church activities. But, you may have to make some adjustments as far as the time you can spend on your commitments, and you may need to reorganize your priorities. But if God called you to something before you had a child, He hasn't changed His mind after you've had it. There will be a change in your schedule; it's going to take more time to get out of the house. You will need to spend time with your child (especially nursing mothers). You will still have friends and other people to serve; you will still be living the same lifestyle you did before the baby came. You won't want to devote yourself totally to your new child to the exclusion of other people and other areas of your life.

NURSING

Some women question whether or not to nurse their children. It seems to be quite controversial. There are books around that will tell you either way is the only way, and that there will be negative side effects for you and your child if you choose the "wrong" way. I believe that God has given women a tremendous gift to be able to nurse their children. It is a very special time of sharing and closeness with your new child that is irreplaceable. Besides the benefits of providing the best food for your child, there is also the amount of time you spend loving that child. Being able to hold, talk, pray, and sing to your child is such a benefit. No matter how busy you are, you have to slow down, relax and take time to feed your baby. It is very special and important for your child to know you are there.

I think the biggest problem women have when it comes to nursing is just plain being uptight about it. The best thing you can do is relax. Remember, this is what God made you to do. If God did not want you to nurse He wouldn't have equipped your body for that purpose. It's a normal function of your body. Many times women worry about whether they will have enough milk, if their milk is good enough, or if the baby is eating enough. If you relax and stop worrying, your body will have enough milk, and you'll have no problem. You need to tell yourself that it is no big deal. If you have a relaxed attitude, your body will release the pressure and tension that comes from thinking, "I'm supposed to do this, and I'm supposed to do that." Your body can begin to tighten up because of worry, and stop all the good things that would just come naturally. If the thought comes to you that you won't be able to nurse your child, you can say, "Wait a minute, God has given me this gift as woman." As a woman, you've been given the ability in your body to nurse your child. It is a natural function in your body. Don't allow anyone or anything to rob you of this special gift.

When your first baby is born, you are new to it all. You've never done this before, and because of this most women go through the same insecurities and doubts. They wonder if they are doing things right, and how someone else would do it, and many times they just feel unprepared for the things that come up. I would like to share a few tips with you about nursing.

1. Babies are born knowing how to suck. You don't have to worry about whether or not they

will be able to nurse.

2. Attempt to nurse immediately (at least within the first 20-30 minutes). This helps the baby calm down. It also causes the mother's uterus to contract to help deliver the placenta and start milk production.

3. The child and mother should not be separated during the first few hours. God planned for part of the birthing process to be a bonding time for a new relationship, a time for the new mother and child to get to know each other.

4. The baby's facial muscles are developed through nursing. Their cheeks are designed to nurse. Some experts say there are definite physical benefits for babies who nurse. Bottle-feeding doesn't provide the same exercise and the child doesn't develop the same way as those who nurse.

5. It has been said the mother's body will get back into physical condition much easier after nursing. God is very smart in how He has planned for us to work with our bodies.

6. Prepare your body ahead of time. Since this is new it is very wise to do some simple things to prepare yourself physically. You'll be very glad you did.

   a. Prepare your nipples by doing this simple exercise each day: grasp your nipple between your thumb and forefinger; gently pull it until it stings slightly.

   b. After your shower each day, spend a minute briskly rubbing your nipples with a slightly rough towel.

   c. Do not wear your bra whenever possible. This will also help to toughen up your nipples.

7. Once your milk starts coming in, it will take a while for your body to learn to control it. During the first few weeks, you may have milk leak at different times. (That's why you need to stock up on those amazing nursing pads!)

8. Schedule consistent feeding times, and stick with it. Feeding a baby every time he cries or demands something is training him to be very

undisciplined in his eating habits. Set a schedule of feeding for every three to four hours and then stick to it. This is a very positive discipline. You are helping yourself and also helping your child.

9. If you have a problem with nursing, such as sore, cracked nipples, don't give up! Tell yourself you'll nurse for one more week. Every woman I know who has done this has been successful in overcoming the situation.

One thing I have found with many of the women I have been around is they have difficulty nursing because of nutritional or physical challenges they are having themselves. Make sure you are eating properly. Make sure what you are eating is the best nutritionally for you to be able to properly feed your little one. If you need to add something more to your diet or stay away from certain foods for a period of time, just make the decision to do it and to be happy about it.

Remember, this time period is very short. It may

seem like certain seasons of life go on forever, but as a mom of young adults I have to say it is really very short and goes by very quickly. This time is all about nurturing a healthy, strong child, not about certain visions or goals we may have set up.

There are many good books to read for more "how-to's" regarding nursing techniques, positioning and breast care during nursing. The more knowledge we have, the better we are able to succeed. Get wisdom and allow yourself to change as needed. Don't get stuck into feeling like you need to perform or do what someone else has done.

CHAPTER 12

ENTRUSTING YOUR CHILD TO THE LORD

I think one of the most important things that you can settle within yourself about having a baby – the pregnancy, the delivery, and the first few months – is that God is helping you. He cares about you and your child. And since God cares about you, you don't need to be uptight and scared about anything. Everyone goes through the same basic situations you are experiencing. If you'll talk and communicate with "elder" women who have handled that particular situation, you will have greater knowledge and confidence to handle each challenge that comes along. Every new parent and child goes through little changes. With one baby, it might be the flu; with another baby, it might be a fever. Things are going to come up occasionally, but we need to have it settled that they are not going to overwhelm us, and we will overcome the obstacles.

Don't allow fear, worry, or doubt to control any situation that comes up during your pregnancy or as a new parent. You can believe God for the protection and care of your child. Psalm 91 is excellent to meditate on and confess over your children. The

Word of God is more powerful than any negative circumstance that would try to come against your family. With all the little things that can come up, don't panic, get nervous, or wonder what you did wrong. Confess God's Word, pray in faith, and talk to friends. The wisdom of God is working in you, so be confident that you will make the right decisions. Remember, if God is for us, who can be against us? (Romans 8:31)

CHAPTER 13

OTHER TESTIMONIES
OF SUCCESS

Although there were fifteen years between my first two children, both of my pregnancies were very similar. I fought a great deal with "morning sickness." I had it morning, noon, and night. The only difference was that I had become a Christian with my second child and had been learning the Word of God concerning health and healing. Because of the promises of God I began to renew my mind about morning sickness and by the end of my second pregnancy, I was feeling much better than I had during my first pregnancy.

My husband and I decided early in the second pregnancy that we would have our baby at home with the help of a few friends. My labor and delivery went very well.

Although the labor wasn't extremely quick, it was very smooth. I walked and prayed by myself for the first few hours, since it was the middle of the night. At about 3:30am, I called one of my friends to come over. We walked and talked together for the next five hours.

Before I knew it, it was time to deliver. Our baby

came out easily after three or four good pushes. There she was, eight pounds, six ounces and 20¾ inches long. What a beautiful girl! It was a special time! I felt God's presence there with us. He certainly knows how to give good gifts (Psalm 127:3).

I had to use my faith and fight the good fight throughout my pregnancy with our daughter, and I prayed and believed God for His Word to work in my life. Even while I was still pregnant with our daughter, I was confessing out of my mouth that I would not be sick with my next baby. Hurray! I was not sick at all with the third pregnancy! Having babies God's way is the best. Believe His Word, it will work for you.

By S. B.

I had my first child in 1984. After 12 hours of hard labor, the doctors said the baby's head was too big to fit through my pelvis, and they took him by caesarean section. The doctors said I could never have a baby vaginally because my pelvis was extremely small and abnormally shaped. I knew God intended childbirth to be a beautiful, natural experience, so I prayed and began to confess that I would have a natural delivery next time.

Two years later, I became pregnant for the second time. When I was two months along, I went in to the doctor for a check up. He confirmed what had been said about my pelvis and told me the largest baby I would ever be able to deliver naturally would only weigh three pounds. After this, I was in a meeting with Wendy and a few other sisters who laid hands on me and prayed that my pelvis would be made right. The next doctor that examined me said I was normal and she would give me a trial "Vaginal Birth After Caesarian" (VBAC)!

The next thing I found out was that I was carrying twins. This really complicated my chances of delivering naturally, so the doctor gave me these qualifications: both babies had to be head down, they could not weigh more than five pounds each, and there could not be any complications, such as fetal distress. I began praying that I would have great favor with the doctors no matter how big the babies were, and for them to be healthy and strong.

Around my sixth month, I started to have pre-term labor. Friends from church agreed with me that I would not "cast my fruit before its time" – specifically March 2nd, the end of my eighth month. On March 2nd, I went into active labor! Both babies were in head down position and their weight was estimated to be about five pounds each, just like my doctor had wanted. However, my doctor went off duty, and her partner took over my delivery. My daughter was born naturally after just four and one-half hours. She weighed six pounds, seven and one-half ounces and her head was only one-half inch smaller than my first child whose head was "too big"! Then we discovered that the second twin was now feet first and was in some distress. Now I found out why God had given me the partner instead of my doctor. Instead of giving me an emergency C-section, as my doctor had stated, this doctor confidently guided the baby with his hands to speed up the delivery. My six pound, thirteen and one-half ounce son was born breech just a few minutes later. After the birth, the nurses and other delivery room attendants realized they had never seen a VBAC birth with twins before, much less a completely natural one. Someone said, "You deserve a standing ovation!" and they all clapped. But all the praise really goes to our Father, Who performed miracle after miracle to bring forth these two beautiful babies.

By L. B.

We have four beautiful, healthy, happy boys. The first three pregnancies and deliveries were good, but because of lack of knowledge of God's Word, we put up with fear, negative physical symptoms, and long, intense labors. But by the fourth pregnancy we had grown in God's love and His Word enough to know it was not His perfect will for us to suffer in any way.

At first, my wife knew she was pregnant because

of the nausea, which was what always happened the first three months of her pregnancies. After a few weeks of accepting it, we decided that it had no place in our lives. We prayed together in agreement and began to fight it. Within a few days, it was gone! For the remainder of her pregnancy we continued to speak the Word of God over my wife and our child, and we allowed no more negative symptoms to stay.

The night my wife went into labor, we had just gone to bed when her water broke. It was 9:45pm. We knew this labor would be different because her water had never broken before until she was ready to deliver. We had the friend come over who was going to assist us with our child's birth, and we made all our preparations for the delivery. She continued to have good, strong contractions as she walked, prayed, and played Scrabble in between. At 2:25am, she began to have enough pressure that it was no longer comfortable to walk or stand. Within twenty minutes and three or four good pushes, our beautiful healthy son was born! What a glorious moment!

Commitment to and trust in God's Word made this pregnancy different from the others. We encourage you to consider these things carefully and move in confidence towards God's best for you. He is faithful to His Word!

By H. W.

One year ago, I met a pastor from Christian Faith Center while I was a counselor at summer camp. At the time, my husband and I were in the process of starting the paperwork to adopt a child. I had already had three miscarriages, but we wanted to start a family. I know God specifically led me to this camp to meet this pastor. After we talked and prayed, I was really built up and encouraged to have faith in God's power.

Shortly after that I became pregnant. As we awaited the arrival of our little girl, Satan did his best to shake our faith. When I was 14 weeks along, I began to hemorrhage. My husband and I took authority over the devil and commanded him to go in the Name of Jesus. The bleeding stopped that same day! Every time thereafter when Satan attempted an attack, we just took authority over it! We gave birth to a six pound, four ounce baby girl. It was the most wonderful experience of my life! Praise God!

By D.W.

Do you need prayer regarding your pregnancy or delivery? We have believers who want to pray with you for any aspect of childbirth. Please let us know your need, whatever it may be through the contact information below:

Casey Treat Ministries

PO Box 98800

Seattle, Washington 98198

www.caseytreat.com; www.wendytreat.com

or

info@caseytreat.org

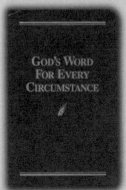

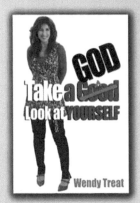

Made in United States
Troutdale, OR
04/07/2024

19030233R00086